GUIDE BOOK FOR WATERCOLOR PAINTING

I0490585

Practical manual for making over 12 watercolor painting designs

Charles N. Howard

Table of Contents

CHAPTER ONE..3

INTRODUCTION...3

CHAPTER TWO 7

METHODOLOGY OF PAINTING.............7

CHAPTER THREE...19

CREATING SHAPES THROUGH
PAINTING...19

CHAPTER ONE

INTRODUCTION

Watercolor painting is the use of watercolor in painting and designing objects. Any artwork work that is created by using the usage of the use of watercolor as a medium is identified as watercolor art. Most watercolor artworks are watercolor paintings.

However, watercolor is moreover used in illustrations, drawings, and blended media artworks. The watercolor medium has been spherical for a prolonged time and dates as a lengthy way once more as the Stone Age. It is a stunning medium allowing greater than a few probabilities of expression.

Trace of watercolor to present age

Watercolor art work refers to any works of art work made the utilization of the medium of watercolor. Watercolor moreover refers to the medium, a water-soluble paint that has apparent or translucent properties. Many human beings describe watercolors as being tender or mild due to the reality the pigments in watercolors are often no longer as brilliant as acrylics or oil paints. Watercolor consists of pigment particles blended with a binder from natural sources like gum, glucose, and glycerin. It is water-soluble.

Watercolors are provided as cakes of baked color or as a liquid in containers, in which water is blended for activation. Watercolors are non-toxic and included as in distinction to unique mediums, such as oil paints.

Essential tools and equipment in watercolor painting

If you want to paint with watercolor, first rate paper is very important. Without actual paper, painting will in no way obtain its full potential. Poor paper extraordinary will have an impact on even the exceptional artist's work. Another element to take into account is that when we use this medium, we are the utilization of water.

This capacity that our paper needs to be face up to the water and now not warp, Using scotch or defending tape to maintain your paper down will aid preserve the complete lot in neighborhood and prevent your paper from shifting.

CHAPTER TWO

METHODOLOGY OF PAINTING

What is Lifting in watercolor painting?

Lifting is a really useful watercolor technique when one needs to make horrible residence to paint inside or to create results such as clouds or moderate marks. This specific strategy consists of in truth lifting the paint from your paper's surface.

How to use Dark Effect in Painting

Usually, when we paint, we start in slight and end in dark. This is what makes this watercolor method so specific we do it the opposite way, in different words; we use the darker color until now than the lighter one. You can start by using the usage of as quickly as soon as extra coating your demarcated block with a skinny water layer.

What is Gradient in watercolor Painting?

Our subsequent watercolor technique is a positive watercolor basic. A simple, however efficient, gradient, whilst you can additionally consider it is very easy; in order to create a seamless gradient does require suitable technique. Your full attentiveness is desired and, if you do it correctly, you want to be left with an amazing result.

Area to use gradients

Gradients are recommended when painting horizons, sunsets, or panorama backgrounds especially. This watercolor have an impact on is an organization favored and helps create the first-class galaxy. It is exciting to do and works very exact when painting with watercolors.

The use of Salt in Watercolor mixture

Head to the kitchen and take maintain of some salt to hold close this terrific and fun watercolor technique. Often, the quality consequences can be performed by way of way of the use of objects that are no longer typically in your artist's closet. If you wish to paint parts or even snowflakes falling, the salt technique will be suitable up your alley.

Guide In Painting Using Wet-On-Wet

Make a wet in rectangles

There are a couple of easy techniques to paint with watercolor.

The wet-on-wet approach is generally used for painting landscapes, effortless skies, or clean watercolor washes due to the reality they have an impact on provides us an brilliant glide appear to be that can be utilized in wonderful ways. Start with the aid of wetting your brush with easy water and portray two rectangles.

Pick moist paint and add color

The rectangles will be challenging to see due to the truth there's no pigment, on the other hand if you tilt your head a bit, you will see the vicinity you have utilized the water. Pick up moistened paint from your palette and add color to your moist rectangle.

Slide brush and gauge

In this image, I'm surely sliding my brush from factor to side. In your 2nd rectangle, clearly add dabs of paint. This assignment is brilliant for moving forward to gauge the volume of water and paint you determine on to use.

Allow it to dry

Next, your paint has begun to dry. When painting wet-on-wet, we don't have a lousy lot manipulate over how our paint reacts. This is a gorgeous thing of this technique; watercolor dries in mysterious ways.

After dry up, observed the textures content

Once the paint has definitely dried, you'll see that it's modified even more. It's every day for colors to exhibit up a whole lot much less vivid as quickly as they've dried. Interesting textures moreover show up which makes wet-on-wet an incredible technique for which include texture to painted shapes.

How To Paint Blooms

Pre-wet and mix palette

A region of your paper with effortless water the utilization of a massive brush and going over the neighborhood at least 2-5 cases to arrive at an even sheen, Swivel your paintbrush in your container of water to pre-wet it, and load it with nice, juicy coloration you have prepared on your mixing palette.

Dip brush in water and apply

Touch the tip of your brush to the ground of the water. Allow the coloration to drop from the brush onto the water. Repeat until you have carried out the appreciated effect. Allow the bloom to dry beforehand than together with greater colorations or details.

Let it dry and use a good paper

Different kinds of paper soak up water differently, and this can have an effect on your painting. Choose a good-quality watercolor paper that is thick enough to retain the water except buckling or warping, when painting watercolor blooms, it is essential to use a slight touch. This will help end the paint from spreading to an entire lot and ruining your painting. And remember, you can continuously add higher paint if you prefer to, then again it is a lot extra challenging to dispose of paint as quickly as it is on the paper.

Assemble color and blooms

So start with a moderate contact and then assemble up the color progressively until you get the have an impact on you is looking for. Add water sparingly, Too a lot water can cause the paint to run and make your blooms show up muddy. Add water sparingly, and completely when necessary, to maintain away from this problem. If you do through accident add too a lousy lot water, simply blot the greater moisture with a paper towel. Be cautious now no longer to rub the paint too hard, or you will cease up with a blurry bloom.

Add in variations and intermix

Use different colors for variation; one of the magnificent matters about watercolor blooms is that you can use any coloration you want. To add hobby and variation utilization of two or three colors then again of actual one, you can moreover scan with awesome color combos to see what you like best. Just take notice to continue to be interior a same color family so that you no longer danger create a color you do now not want when they commence intermixing.

CHAPTER THREE

CREATING SHAPES THROUGH PAINTING

Wreath Watercolor Paint

Material use

Paper

Paint

Brush

Tissue and Water Jar

Create spherical shape and draw

Use any spherical object like a bowl and trace outline with pencil to create a notable spherical shape. Try to draw gently so that the pencil plan won't be obvious in the closing painting.

Brush and create petals

Start with the shade Seaside or a turquoise color. We will be portraying 4 petal flowers. Start with the resource of making use of moderate pressure on your brush and slowly press the belly of the brush on the paper to create petal shapes. Paint some different petal beside the first petal. Paint two greater petals to complete the three petal flower.

Center wet and creates design

While the flower is nevertheless wet, snatch a pigmented aggregate of indigo and drop it in the center of the flower. This will create an exceptional big difference in the core of the flower.

Paints the shapes created

Continue painting increased plants in exquisite colorings of blue. This will make your painting show up greater charming and desirable to the eyes. Once you have set up a few for petal flowers, you can also moreover try together with some filler petals. They can be surely two petals. The petal shapes don't desire to appear perfect. Once they are painted together in a group, you won't see the imperfections. Try such as vegetation that are pigmented and put it beside a flower that seems diminished or moderate colored.

Fill up and add leaves

Now that we have filled half of the wreath with mini flowers, can now add some leaves. Paint the leaves alternately on the pencil outline. Also, include one of variety shades of green. You may additionally moreover add a higher diluted sap inexperienced or a greenish yellow color. Add Indigo to Sap Green to create a deeper shade of green.

Paints leave and close gap

Completed with the pinnacle side of the wreath, paint the leaves at the bottom side. That the pinnacle and bottom aspect will meet in the middle. Close the gap between the pinnacle and bottom leaves.

Strokes fill and make layers

You may additionally overlap the leaves to make it appear seamless. In this wreath, we painted the leaves in two directions; on the other hand journey free to paint it in one direction. Begin filling some gaps with small skinny strokes like this. It will surely show up like stems sticking out. Wait for the first layer of leaves to dry beforehand than painting some different layer of leaves. This method will produce a wreath with greater extent and lots much less gaps between the leaves. For the second layer, use a higher diluted inexperienced paint.

Add more filler and end up

This is output of layering the leaves. To take a look at if the wreath is complete, keep your painting some distance away from you or take an image and appear to be at it on your phone. This is to change the way you see the wreath. For this photo, add more flowers. Add filler petals to make the flower place appear fuller. Add some leaves in between the flowers, Finished.

Sunset Watercolor Paint

Material use

Paintbrushes

300GSM paper

Watercolor pan paint

Ruler

Masking tape

A coin

Instructions guide

Create pages

When painting a watercolor sunset, don't decide upon in equal halves. This is due to the truth the ratio of water to sky wants to by way of no potential be even as it normally has a greater aesthetic look.

Create segment of sun

Try to divide actually beneath halfway with some scotch tape. The coin is going to create a horrible place that will be the brightest segment of the sun.

Dip brush water and paint

With water on our brush, maintain your finger pressed down onto the coin. Then begin to add water spherical that coin with your brush. That circle region to be dry so that as add color it will naturally repel from going into the dry area.

After dry, add layers and stokes

Add first layer of the sunset which can be any slight coloration such as yellow. Add some highlights of orange into your already present day mix of yellow. Then proceed to make some strokes in your sky with your orange coloration to create a gesture of moody clouds. Sunsets are in no way the equal so trip free to make all sorts of marks at the identical time as the paper is however wet.

Make a transfer and liner strokes

Whilst the sky is on the other hand wet, begin to be playful with color combos that you may additionally select to exist in your sunset. For example, a proper wondering is to slowly assemble from your yellow to darker tones transferring from reds to blues and purples. Follow these pretty a range colors in the sky. Assume about squiggle motions and linear strokes to imitate one of a kind sorts of cloud structures. Sunset in watercolor can be without a doubt stunning as the medium water excellent approves for a lot of easy gradient shifts.

Shades and water paints

Try to be swift and quote your utility of new shades at the identical time as the net web page is then again wet. This will allow for the shades to merge higher seamlessly. Try to moreover now not dominate the lighter tones with your darker tones in your sundown water painting. Including the darker tones inner the corners of our sky, this allows for suitable big difference barring the lighter colorings being actually dominated.

Inners paint the sky

Once your sky has honestly dried, we have to be left with a captivating color variant inner the sky aspect of our painting. What we can do now is slowly and gently elevates the overlaying tape off from the core of our page.

Avoid overlap

Take a new piece of defending tape or scotch tape and start to region it horizontally onto net web page predominantly over the painted half of our page. However, a moderate overlap of the scotch tape on the empty part of the page. A slight overlap of scotch tape located horizontally onto the internet web page the location there would be a horizon line. This little overlap of the scotch tape is going to create a silver lining on the horizon that helps to distinguish the two elements of our painting.

Paint Water Reflection and moist brush

Scotch tape placed down horizontally on our page, we have to have an average overlap of the scotch tape positioned on the issue of the vicinity we will paint the water. We can then proceed to take a handy moist brush and prim with a bit of water. Paint little skinny horizontal strokes straight away in line with the solar and the area its reflections would exist on the water.

The reflection of the photo voltaic is normally at as soon as under it on the flooring of the water. Imitate the equal coloration qualities of our sky; this is regularly a more sensible illustration of how reflections in the water work with sunsets.

Stokes spherical and paint yellow strokes

Via way of painting little yellow strokes spherical a vertical awful residence left unpainted that falls straight away underneath the sun. Leave this negative 2nd of unpainted paper going for walks down the vertically at as soon as underneath your sun.

Proceed to paint yellow strokes barely overlapping into this bad vicinity of the internet web page to furnish the have an effect on of waves. You can moreover paint the leisure of the yellow spherical this horrific space.

Adding Darker Tones in the Water While the wet, begin to add some horizontal strokes of orange in the water. Imitate the coloration nice of the sky; add horizontal strokes due to the reality it creates the characteristics of ripples in the water.

End up

Color variant inner our sky that is mirrored interior the water in the bottom section of our painting, Once painting is dry we can begin to get rid of the masking tape on our horizon line.